NEW MUSICAL EXPR

POLL WINNERS CONC

"IF SOMEONE THINKS
THAT LOVE AND PEACE
IS A CLICHÉ THAT MUST
HAVE BEEN LEFT BEHIND
IN THE '60S, THAT'S THEIR
PROBLEM. LOVE AND
PEACE ARE ETERNAL"

CONTENTS

A Mirror publication
Marketing Manager: Fergus McKenna
Mirrorpix: David Scripps and Alex Waters
020 7293 3858

Produced by Trinity Mirror Sport Media, PO BOX 48, Liverpool L69 3EB. 0151 227 2000

Executive Editor: Ken Rogers **Senior Editor:** Steve Hanrahan **Senior Art Editor:** Rick Cooke **Editor:** Paul Dove
Compiled and written by: Alan Jewell **Sub Editor:** James Cleary
Design: Matthew Barnes, Zoe Bevan, Colin Harrison
Part of the Mirror Collection © Published by Trinity Mirror
Images: Mirrorpix, Trinity Mirror, PA Photos, Apple Corps, Associated Press,
Camera Press, Capitol Records, London Features International, MJS
Printed: by PCP

HE STILL SHINES ON

The shooting of John Lennon in December 1980 robbed the world of one of its most popular singers, shortly after he emerged from a five-year musical hibernation. His loss is still felt greatly by those who grew up with the Beatles, and many who weren't even born when he died. He left behind a body of work that remains a soundtrack to our lives

Thirty years have passed since his sudden, shocking, senseless murder, but John Lennon continues to intrigue and inspire.

Singer, songwriter, poet, peace campaigner, controversialist…Lennon, an icon of the 20th century, remains a source of fascination into the 21st.

There surely can't be a deceased artist whose songs are heard so regularly in Britain, whether from the Beatles era or his solo years between 1970 and 1980.

EMI are releasing digitally remastered versions of Lennon's albums to mark what would have been his 70th birthday. The 'Gimme Some Truth' catalogue is being overseen by his widow, Yoko Ono.

His legacy surrounds us still. Passengers flying into his home city of Liverpool land at John Lennon Airport, renamed in his honour in 2002.

Also in Liverpool, Lennon's childhood home, 251 Menlove Avenue, is owned by the National Trust and open to the public. In 2009 Bob Dylan, in the city for a concert, joined unsuspecting tourists on one of the guided tours, keen to see where one of his contemporaries grew up.

A memorial garden, Strawberry Fields, is situated in New York's Central Park, across the road from the Dakota building, the Lennons' home from 1973 and the site of his murder in 1980.

Since it opened in 1985, Strawberry Fields has become a place of pilgrimage for Lennon fans, peace campaigners and people seeking quiet contemplation. Flowers and memorabilia are often placed on the 'Imagine' mosaic. It becomes a particular focal point on the anniversary of his birth (October 9) and death (December 8).

Three decades have now passed since his life was snuffed out late on a Monday night in New York City.

At about 5pm on that fateful evening, Lennon autographed his new album, 'Double Fantasy', for a man stood outside the Dakota, as he left and headed to a recording studio with Yoko.

The man was Mark David Chapman, who waited for Lennon's return. When he did reappear, shortly before 11pm, Chapman called out, crouched into the combat stance and shot Lennon four times. He was rushed to the nearby Roosevelt Hospital in a police car, but was pronounced dead at 11.07.

The news broke quickly. In his adopted home of America, millions heard of the assassination while watching the final seconds of an NFL game between the Miami Dolphins and the New England Patriots. Commentator Howard Cosell, who had interviewed Lennon on the 'Monday Night Football' programme six years earlier, stunned viewers when he announced "an unspeakable tragedy".

With Britain five hours ahead of New York, Lennon's death occurred before dawn. Night-shift workers were the first to hear, as radio broadcasts were interrupted by the news and Lennon songs took over the airwaves.

Disbelieving, distraught fans began to congregate at the Dakota and for days afterwards a sea of mourners filled 72nd Street. There was sobbing, singing and chanting from some; stunned silence from others.

The dream was over. One of the four lads who shook the world had departed it way, way before his time.

Yoko Ono announced there would be no funeral and instead asked for a silent vigil on the following Sunday, which was observed all over the world but particularly in New York and Liverpool, where huge crowds gathered at Central Park and St George's Hall.

Left: John and his soulmate, Yoko Ono. This picture was released to publicise 'The John Lennon Anthology'

The Fab Four:
December 1963

Although his life had been prematurely cut short, Lennon packed an incredible amount into his 40 years.

Largely brought up by his Aunt Mimi, he was an artistic but disruptive presence at school. His first band was 'The Quarrymen', formed in 1957. In July of that year they played at a church fete in Woolton, Liverpool. Another music-obsessed teenager, Paul McCartney, was present and the seed of a musical revolution was sown.

The Quarrymen morphed into 'The Silver Beetles' and, finally, 'The Beatles'. Their sound was developed while playing at The Cavern Club in Liverpool and during tours of Hamburg, West Germany. By 1962 the line-up settled at: Lennon, McCartney, George Harrison and Ringo Starr.

In the same year Lennon married his long-term girlfriend Cynthia Powell after she fell pregnant. By the time their son, Julian, was born in April 1963, the Beatles were experiencing the early stages of chart success in Britain. John Lennon was now public property.

The group's popularity grew and grew and by the latter months of '63 the word 'Beatlemania' had entered the lexicon. This phenomenon spread across the Atlantic in February 1964 when they went to America for the first time.

Lennon was caught in a whirlwind of song-writing, recording, touring and filming. The level of hysteria was unprecedented.

A stunned crowd surround the Dakota building as word spreads that John Lennon has been shot dead. To the right, the lyrics to 'Imagine', his most famous song. Opposite, the Daily Mirror front page from December 10, 1980

By 1966, something had to give. Screaming was drowning out the sound of the Beatles' public performances and there were no more commercial concerts after a show at San Francisco's Candlestick Park in August. Lennon was also shaken by the controversy that ensued when he casually remarked that "we're more popular than Jesus now".

Despite their demanding schedule, the Lennon-McCartney partnership was flourishing and classic song followed classic song. The music was becoming more experimental and complex, garnering popular and critical acclaim.

Lennon's life was soon to undergo fundamental changes. The death of Beatles' manager Brian Epstein in August 1967 was arguably the beginning of the end for the group. Less than 12 months later he and Cynthia separated and Japanese avant-garde artist Yoko Ono became his partner.

They married in March 1969 and announced an upcoming "happening", which proved to be their first bed-in, where they promoted world peace. They soon formed the 'Plastic Ono Band' and began releasing music, notably the anthemic 'Give Peace A Chance'. His MBE, awarded to all the Beatles in 1965, was returned to the Queen in protest at the Vietnam War and Biafra conflict.

Lennon left the Beatles in 1969, although the end for the group wasn't confirmed until McCartney spoke publicly about his musical and business differences with his erstwhile partner in April 1970.

In December Lennon released his first solo album, followed less than a year later by his second, 'Imagine'. 'Some Time In New York City' (which was now his home) came out in 1972, 'Mind Games' in 1973, 'Walls and Bridges' in 1974 and 'Rock 'N' Roll' in 1975.

DAILY Mirror

SPECIAL ISSUE

Wednesday, December 10, 1980   12p

JOHN LENNON shot dead in New York Dec 8 1980

DEATH OF A HERO

MURDERED SUPERSTAR: One of the last pictures of ex-Beatle John Lennon, taken in New York three weeks ago.

PLEASE TURN TO PAGES TWO AND THREE

The two women in Lennon's life: with first wife Cynthia in 1964. On the opposite page, a hug for Yoko in London, 1971

The first half of the '70s were a prolific and turbulent period in his life. He and Yoko continued to campaign for peace and their criticism of the Vietnam War drew a sharp response from the paranoid Nixon administration, which, in early 1972, attempted to deport him on the basis of a 1968 drugs conviction in Britain. Lennon took the case to court and a four-year legal battle followed before he was eventually given a Green Card in 1976.

In 1973 Lennon and Ono became estranged and, on his wife's suggestion, he began a relationship with their personal assistant, May Pang. They moved to Los Angeles and his 18-month 'lost weekend' began. Often sharing the company of Harry Nilsson and producer Phil Spector, he was frequently drunk and out of control.

Although Lennon released plenty of music in the early '70s, live appearances were few and far between. His final headlining show was a charity concert at New York's Madison Square Garden in August 1972, although he appeared live one more time at the same venue in November 1974. Elton John had performed on 'Whatever Gets You Thru The Night' and when it went to number one in the USA, Lennon honoured a promise to join Elton on stage during one of his shows at MSG.

In the audience that night was Yoko and she and Lennon met afterwards. This was the catalyst for their reunion, which was confirmed in early 1975.

Yoko, who was 42 in February '75, soon became pregnant. She had suffered three miscarriages previously but there was to be no more heartbreak and baby Sean was born on October 9, John's 35th birthday.

At this point Lennon effectively retreated from public life and became a full-time house-husband, caring for Sean during the day while Yoko looked after their business interests. Five years passed without any new tunes. He even remarked that he had made his contribution to civilisation.

While on holiday in Bermuda in June 1980, the urge to make music returned. The 'Double Fantasy' album was recorded at 'The Hit Factory' in New York in August and September. Lead single '(Just Like) Starting Over' was released in October.

Guitarist Earl Slick said of the Double Fantasy sessions: "He was excited about everything all the time. Every song that we did, the idea of putting a new record out, the idea of touring – everything he talked about was definitely with a tone of excitement."

The tour, planned for 1981, would never come to pass. We can only guess what Lennon would have got up to in the past 30 years, had he lived. But why waste time speculating about what might have been when there is so much to remember him by.

Singles

1969:
Give Peace A Chance: UK no. 2
Cold Turkey: UK no. 14

1970:
Instant Karma: UK no. 5

1971:
Power To The People: UK no. 7

1972:
Woman Is The Nigger of the World: Did not chart in the UK
Happy Xmas (War Is Over): UK no. 4 (reached no. 3 in December 1980)

1973:
Mind Games: UK no. 26

1974:
Whatever Gets You Thru The Night: UK no. 36 (no. 1 in the USA)

1975:
No. 9 Dream: UK no. 23
Stand By Me: UK no. 30
Imagine: UK no. 6 (Lennon's most famous song was released as a single in the USA in 1971, four years before the UK. It went to no. 1 in January 1981 following his death)

1980:
(Just Like) Starting Over: UK no. 1

1981:
Woman: UK no. 1
Watching The Wheels: UK no. 30

1982:
Love/Gimme Some Truth: UK no. 41

1984:
Nobody Told Me: UK no. 6
Borrowed Time: UK no. 32
I'm Stepping Out: UK no. 55
Every Man Has A Woman Who Loves Him: Did not chart in UK

1985:
Jealous Guy: UK no. 65

Studio albums:
Plastic Ono Band (1970)
Imagine (1971)
Some Time In New York City (1972)
Mind Games (1973)
Walls And Bridges (1974)
Rock 'N' Roll (1975)
Double Fantasy (1980)
Milk And Honey (1984)

Compilations:
Shaved Fish (1975)
The John Lennon Collection (1982)
Imagine (1988)
Lennon Legend (1997)
The John Lennon Anthology (1998)
Working Class Hero: The Definitive Lennon (2005)

THE BEATLES YEARS

A rock 'n' roll group who grew out of Liverpool in the late 1950s and early '60s changed the course of music history. The figurehead of the band was John Winston Lennon

Beatlemania: Night of triumph for four young men at the Royal Variety Show

Tuesday, November 5, 1963

Leading Beatle John Lennon bawled into the microphone at the Royal Variety Show last night:

"Those in the cheaper seats please clap – and the rest of you rattle your jewellery."

The 1,200 people in the audience at the Prince of Wales Theatre – seats from one to twenty guineas – cheered and clapped approvingly.

And the four lucky lads from Liverpool were IN. They had broken down the show's traditional "stuffed-shirt" barrier.

From then on the usually sedate audience made it quite clear that they had been bitten by the Beatle bug. And that they were ENJOYING it.

As the group swept into its first number – 'From Me To You' – the theatre rocked as hands clapped and feet stamped.

In the royal box Princess Margaret, in a red and gold brocade down, was snapping her fingers in time with the music.

The Queen Mother smiled happily – and clapped with the rest of 'em.

The Beatlemania fever increased with the group thumping their hearts out with 'She Loves You' (Yeah, Yeah, Yeah), 'Twist and Shout' and 'Till There Was You'.

Last night EVERYBODY loved the Beatles – Yeah, Yeah, Yeah.

Opposite, top: Lennon plays with The Quarrymen in June 1957 on the day he met Paul McCartney
Opposite, bottom: The leather-clad Beatles with Pete Best on drums
Left: John in Portsmouth in November 1963
Below: Meeting actress Julie Christie

Yeah! Yeah! USA

Saturday, February 8, 1964

Five thousand screaming, chanting teenagers – most of them playing truant from school – gave the Beatles a fantastic welcome here today.

More than 100 extra police were on duty to control the crowd as the group's jet landed at the John F. Kennedy Airport.

Pandemonium broke out among the stamping, banner-waving fans as the Beatles – John Lennon, Paul McCartney, George Harrison and Ringo Starr – stepped from the plane.

One policeman who has worked at the airport for 10 years said: "I think the world has gone mad."

Image: George, John, Paul and Ringo in Huddersfield, November 1963

Opposite page: The Beatles conquer the world in 1964. Clockwise: Appearing on the Ed Sullivan Show in New York; a soft drink outside a cafe in Paris; swimming in Miami and on a train to Washington DC with wife Cynthia wearing a dark wig

A Beatle meets dad – after 17 years

Thursday, April 2, 1964

A Beatle met his biggest fan yesterday – his dad.

It was the first time they have met each other in 17 years.

John Lennon was waiting at a West End rendezvous, then walked in. John recognised him at once.

Said Mr Lennon: "Hello, son. It's great to see you after all this time." John shook his father's hand warmly.

They talked for nearly half an hour, mainly about John's reaction to success, and his future plans.

Why the long separation? John's parents parted when he was four years old.

And although he first went to Blackpool to live with his father, it was only a few months later that he returned to his mother.

Six years ago she was killed in a Liverpool road accident.

The reunion ended when Beatles' manager Brian Epstein broke it up.

He reminded John: "Sorry, but we have an appointment with the BBC."

As he left, Mr Lennon said: "I am very happy to have met John again."

I want to hold my tongue!

Friday, April 24, 1964

John Lennon, full-time Beatle, part-time writer and full-time 'Mickey-taker', shocked a shoal of literary and business folk yesterday.

John was the guest of honour at a Foyle's Literary Luncheon in London to mark the publication of his zany book 'In His Own Write'. And in his own right he broke a long tradition – by refusing to make a speech.

There were gasps and shouts of "shame" when chairman Osbert Lancaster said: "He firmly refuses to get up and address you himself."

But John did stand up. He said: "Thank you very much – you have a lucky face." Then he quickly sat down.

After the lunch, writer Sir Alan Herbert, one of the top table guests, said: "His not speaking was a very poor show. I have never known the guest to refuse to speak."

Derek Taylor, a Beatles' representative, said: "At the last moment John decided he would not speak and the Beatles' manager Brian Epstein would stand in.

John autographed dozens of his books and said: "Speechmaking is not my country. I would be embarrassed. Perhaps when I am 40 I'll be able to do things like that. I hope I didn't upset anyone."

Left: With Cynthia at a lunch to celebrate the publication of 'In His Own Write'
Below: John and Cynthia joined by Ringo Starr and his future wife, Maureen Cox (left) on holiday in Tobago. John and Cynthia arrive home (right)
Opposite, top: Being fed by Roy Orbison's wife, Claudette
Opposite, bottom: A playful sword fight with George Harrison during a break in Ireland

On stage in Paris,
June 1964

John Lennon is not so 'brite', says MP

Saturday, June 20, 1964

Beatle John Lennon was said by Tory MP Charles Curran yesterday to be "in a state of pathetic near-illiteracy".

The evidence, according to Mr Curran, is contained in the recently published 'In His Own Write', which is an off-beat collection of poems, humour and drawings.

And Mr Curran, who said that he had never heard the Beatles but had read John's best-selling book, told the House of Commons it seemed to say a great deal about the kind of education John received in Liverpool.

He noted one of the poems, 'Deaf Ted Danoota and Me', and declared: "I think it has literary merits, and will tell you two things about John Lennon.

"One is that he has a feeling for words, and the other that he is in a state of pathetic near-illiteracy.

"Looking at the book, he seemed to have picked up bits of Tennyson and Browning and Robert Louis Stevenson, while listening with one ear to the football results.

"It suggests that here is a boy who ought to have been given the education which would have enabled him to benefit in terms of enjoyment from the talent he appears to have."

Opposite: A crafty fag in Blackpool, August 1964. On the inset pictures, Lennon and McCartney can be seen arriving at the northern premiere of the 'A Hard Day's Night' in Liverpool
Left: Dancing with George Harrison's mum, Louise, July 1964

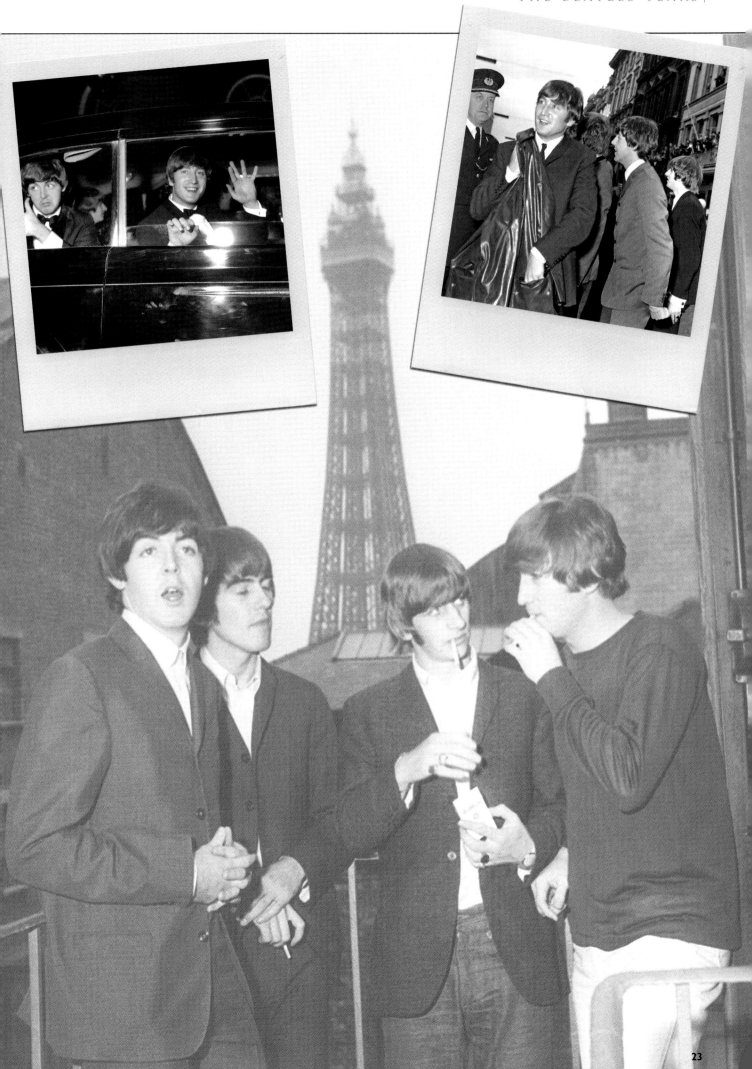

Beatle John in new TV revue

Friday, December 18, 1964

Beatle John Lennon will appear on BBC2 next month – minus George, Ringo and Paul.

He will be reading some of his poems on January 9 in a new revue-type series. Its title: 'Not Only…But Also'.

Regulars in the show will be Dudley Moore and Peter Cook, who were members of the stage show 'Beyond the Fringe' which sparked the British satire wave.

Wrapped up warm while on holiday in St Moritz in January, 1965. Below, a jubilant Lennon celebrates passing his driving test with the other Beatles. On the opposite page, the heartbeat of the group share a microphone

Driver John gets the hit vote

Tuesday, February 16, 1965

John Lennon was telling all the world about passing his driving test yesterday.

Or so it seemed, as scores of Beatles fans watched him tear off his L-plates.

"I'll keep my chauffer," John said. "For the Rolls, of course."

He had passed his test – at Weybridge, Surrey – at the first attempt and after only seven lessons.

John's instructor, Paul Willson, 49, who has been secretly teaching him to drive since Christmas, said: "Mr Lennon was one of the most apt pupils I have had during my 30 years as an instructor."

The one that bites

Donald Zec dissects Mr J Lennon Nassau, Bahamas

Friday, March 5, 1965

It is a lazy day for filming. Ringo is standing under a palm tree and large coconuts are being rhythmically dropped on to his chimney-brush head by a character who appears to be relishing it.

So, too, is Ringo – who knows that at a thousand pounds a clonk this is nice work if you can get it.

True they are cardboard coconuts, but the large dents in them suggest that even the milky real McCoy would bounce brokenly off Mr Starr's shaggy skull.

George and Paul are giggling like monkeys – millionaire monkeys – under a spreading walnut tree, while Eleanor Bron glides ghost-like and barefoot on the hot sand, occasionally murmuring: "I have misgivings about it all."

In short, the second Beatle film is proceeding crazily according to non-plan, and Brian Epstein, as seen through the mosquito mesh of his window, seems a very contented figure – or just very contented with the figures.

This brings me to Mr John Lennon, whose switchblade mind and abrasive throwaway lines make him – for me – the most fascinating Beatle of them all.

Artist, songwriter, author and deep-think extrovert, he is the Beatle that bites.

That head-shrouding hairdo and the faintly idiotic grin suggestive of the slow if not downright retarded can mislead you.

Long conversations with him in this technicoloured paradise have revealed him as a very weighty talent indeed.

With his slow grin and sadly funny appraisal of the square world around him, he resembles a WC Fields of the pop age.

Head back, eyes screwed up over his sun-baked contact lenses, he dissected a Beatle for me with particular emphasis upon what goes on inside John Lennon.

And if you have ever wondered what heaven – or hell – it is to be a Beatle, this far-flung monologue will tell all.

"I suppose that if all this had happened overnight," – he indicated the palm trees and the hovering waiters – "it would have knocked us out.

"But we got broken in gradually. First it was twenty quid, then fifty, then a hundred and, okay, so now I'm a millionaire.

"But I took to it like a dog takes to water. Born to it, I was," he grinned.

"People said to me: 'Don't you find it a problem?' This gives us a laugh. You try having that problem – it doesn't hurt a bit.

"Not that any of us understand what all this money business is about. You should see us at board meetings. It's all we can do to stop giggling like idiots. All this 'I will now read the minutes of the last meeting.' It's a real drag. Mind you, George has got an idea. He knows a bit about cash and Ringo is learning."

"I hear tell," I said, "that you can all be downright rude – and have been."

"Of course we've been rude – but only rude back," he explained. "Have you any clue about the things people say and do to us?

"We're not cruel. We've seen enough tragedy on Merseyside. But when a mother shrieks, 'Just touch him and maybe he will walk again,' we want to run, cry or just empty our pockets.

"It's a great emotional drag, and this is where Paul helps out. He's the diplomat with the soft soap. He can turn on that smile like little May sunshine and we're out of trouble.

"We're a very tight school, the Beatles. We're like a machine that goes boom, boomchick, chickboom, each of us with our own little job to do. We're just like dogs who can hear high-pitched sounds that humans can't.

"We can be talking to some character and, suddenly, if he becomes a drag, we can all put the shutters up, freeze him out and he would never know.

"It's amazing. Like radar. I can pick up Ringo's mood just by looking at him. It's our own mutual protection mechanism. If we didn't have it, we'd fall apart."

"How important is all this screaming to you?" I asked him.

"We need it like a camel needs water or the Black Watch needs the bagpipes. When we don't get it we mope around like we're in a condemned cell. But George, good old George, is the optimist.

"He blames it on the sound or the microphones and keeps us going. That's why we want to make films and write songs – for the time when the screaming stops.

"The moment one of us steps out of line, gets too big for his boots, we send him up so high he's soon back to being human again.

"Believe me, we don't want the Beatles oversold – but we don't want them sold short either. We're going to remain normal if it kills us."

Beatles' army invades Palace

Wednesday, October 27, 1965

It was frenzied…it was fabulous…it was the day the Beatles nearly took over Buckingham Palace, with a wild, screaming army of fans.

Young Prince Andrew, peering out from a high window, had never seen a Royal Investiture to touch it.

There has never been one like it. And the staider sightseers among yesterday's 1,000-strong crowd outside the Palace for Beatles' MBE day hoped there never would be again.

Teenaged girls clambered up the massive wrought-iron gates of the Palace. Down below, 300 swarming fans struggled with police and threatened to storm the courtyard.

As two Guards bands played regimental music, shouts of 'Yeah! Yeah! Yeah!' shattered the decorum. Policemen lost their helmets. Girls lost their shoes.

The Queen's flag was flying from the masthead, but from the scenes outside, the Beatles could have been in command of the Palace.

Beatles fly in to face the storm

Friday, August 12, 1966

Above: Setting off from Heathrow for what proved their final tour, to America in 1966. An angry reception awaited Lennon for his comments about Jesus. The top picture shows the boys at a press conference after receiving their MBEs in October 1965

The Beatles arrived in America last night at the start of their most controversial tour…but there were no incidents – and very little of the usual excitement.

Following remarks alleged to have been made by John Lennon about Christianity, the Ku Klux Klan have threatened to stage demonstrations at Beatles concerts in America.

Radio stations in 'Bible belt' states of the south are boycotting their music.

And before boarding their plane at London Airport – where the group were given their traditional rousing send-off – John Lennon confessed: "I am worried about what has been going on but I am not worried about doing this tour."

Lennon claims he was quoted out of context in a newspaper which reported him as saying that the Beatles are more popular than Jesus and that the Disciples were thick.

A burly official from Nems enterprises, the firm which controls the group's activities, brought the interview at London Airport to an abrupt end.

The Beatles had previously been ordered not to say anything about the controversy.

Look what the barber did to Beatle John

Wednesday, September 7, 1966

John Lennon had an Army-style haircut yesterday. And he simply didn't look like a Beatle any more.

Gone are the sideboards that nearly covered his ears. Gone – well, almost – is that famous fringe.

And all for the sake of a film in which he plays a soldier.

John, 25, lost the locks at 7.30am in a breakfast room of a pub called 'The Inn on the Heath' near Hanover, West Germany.

That is where he is making the film, 'How I Won The War'.

Only a few people – none of them fans – watched as, piece by piece, John's hair fell to the floor.

Then it was all over. The film men were satisfied that at last he looked right for his soldier role.

John looked in a mirror and said: "I'm really quite glad to have it cut. I've got a new face now."

Joker John at the gents

Monday, November 28, 1966

John Lennon, the well-known Beatle, keeps turning up in the oddest places.

Like yesterday, when he could be seen, in top hat and commissionaire's uniform, doing duty among the potted plants outside a certain Soho establishment called 'Gentlemen'.

Turns out it's a nightclub, according to the script of the BBC television comedy series 'Not Only…But Also', which was being filmed there.

Top: Lennon in character as Musketeer Gripweed while filming 'How I Won The War'

Left: Playing a commissionaire for 'Not Only…But Also'

Opposite, top: Attending a fancy dress party thrown by Georgie Fame, January 1967. The other images show the Beatles at the launch of the Sgt Pepper album, May 1967

John drives away from a car paint shop after his Rolls Royce was given a gaudy decoration

Calling after wife Cynthia, who was left on the platform when the group headed to Bangor for a weekend of transcendental meditation, August 1967

Beatle wife Cynthia just misses the Yogi's Mystic Special

Saturday, August 26, 1967

The Beatles' weekend of peaceful transcendental meditation started off in chaos yesterday.

Three of them turned up late for a train at Euston. And John Lennon's wife, Cynthia, got left behind in the scramble.

She stood sobbing on the platform as the train pulled out with John yelling through a window: "Jump, jump!" But railway police held her back.

The Beatles were off to Bangor, North Wales, with the Hindu mystic Maharishi Mahesh Yogi – His Holiness to his followers.

They were so impressed by the Yogi's lecture in London that they cancelled recording dates to go with him.

Paul McCartney arrived on time but with the train six minutes late because of an engine change, there was still no sign of the Lennons, George Harrison and wife Patti, or Ringo Starr.

They ran on to crowded Platform 13 as the train pulled out and jumped into the last compartment – all except for the tearful Mrs Lennon.

Cynthia eventually joined them by car.

From bottom left to right: Arriving home from a Greek holiday in colourful attire; meeting the press ahead of the 'Our World' satellite broadcast where the Beatles premiered 'All You Need Is Love'; reunited with Cynthia in Bangor

31

Epstein dies at 32

Monday, August 28, 1967

Brian Epstein, the man who made the Beatles, is dead.

The Quiet Prince of Pop, who built up a fantastic multi-million pound showbusiness empire, was found dead in bed at his £31,000 London home yesterday afternoon.

He was just 32.

And last night a stunned Paul McCartney, one of the four Liverpool lads who made Epstein their friend, could only say: "This is a great shock. I'm very upset."

Epstein, who always managed to ride the crest of the Merseyside pop wave, was found at about 2.45pm by his Spanish butler.

The butler went to wake him in his second-floor bedroom at the three-storey terrace house in Chapel Street, Belgravia.

He knocked…and knocked again. There was no reply. So the butler raised the alarm and went inside.

The room was in semi-darkness. The curtains were drawn. And Epstein was in bed.

Commander John Lawler, head of the No. 1 district, Metropolitan Police, said: "We are treating this as a sudden death.

"There will probably be a post-mortem examination but this is a matter for the coroner."

Several bottles and medicines were taken from the house, but there was said to be nothing to link them with the cause of death.

Epstein's body left the house in a coffin about 5pm. And soon tributes from pop stars and fans began to flow in from all over the world.

The Beatles, who are in Bangor, North Wales for the mass rally of a meditation society, made immediate plans to return to London.

First to leave was Paul and his actress girlfriend Jane Asher. She held his hand and wept.

Opposite page, top left: Lennon listens intently to the Maharishi. In the main picture he gives his immediate reaction to the death of Beatles' manager Brian Epstein, flanked by George Harrison and Ringo Starr. Above, a glance back on the 'Magical Mystery Tour' bus

Flashbulbs in the face while arriving at the premiere of 'How I Won The War', Piccadilly Circus, October 1967. The top pictures show John and Cynthia at the London Motor Show in the same month

Joined by the other Beatles and respective
partners at the 'How I Won The War' premiere.
Below, with artist Jonathan Hague at the Royal
Institute Gallery, December 1967

Riddle of Lennon marriage

Monday, June 24, 1968

Beatle John Lennon and his wife, Cynthia, have been in touch with solicitors about their marriage.

The Lennons were married six years ago, before the Beatles leapt to fame. They have a five-year-old son, Julian.

Official spokesmen for the group refused to comment yesterday on rumours of a marriage break-up.

The 27-year-old Lennons themselves were not available for comment. Both were away from their £40,000 home on a private estate in Weybridge, Surrey.

John was in Ireland with friends including Ronan O'Rahilly, founder of Radio Caroline, and Japanese sculptress Yoko Ono.

They are expected to return to England today.

Last week John and Yoko, 35, were seen together at the National Theatre in London. John said then that he did not know where his wife was.

Cynthia returned at the weekend from a three-week holiday in Italy with her mother.

Left: At Heathrow ahead of a flight to India and another meeting with the Maharishi, February 1968. George Harrison's then wife, Patti Boyd, is at the front of the queue. Below, a first public appearance with new partner Yoko Ono, attending the opening night of the Old Vic theatre's adaptation of 'In His Own Write'

With Yoko at the opening of the 'You Are Here' exhibition, July 1968

Lennon puts on an art show...with love to Yoko

Tuesday, July 2, 1968

Beatle John Lennon admitted last night that he is in love with Japanese sculptress Yoko Ono.

His six-year marriage to Cynthia Lennon, 27, had not yet legally broken up, he said. "But I don't want to talk about it," he added.

John, also 27, made his declaration of love at London's most off-beat art show.

It was called: 'To Yoko from John Lennon' and consisted of 365 helium-filled balloons, scores of charity collecting boxes and a white-painted sheet of canvas in a tiny room of a West End gallery.

He was asked why he had not dedicated it to someone else – like the Queen.

John replied: "I don't love the Queen like I love Yoko. I do love her. Of course I do."

Asked whether he intended to marry 35-year-old Yoko, he said: "I don't think marriage is the end product of love."

And to questions about whether a separation was planned, he said: "No comment."

Yoko refused to say anything about any marriage plans. All she would say was: "I am very fond of John."

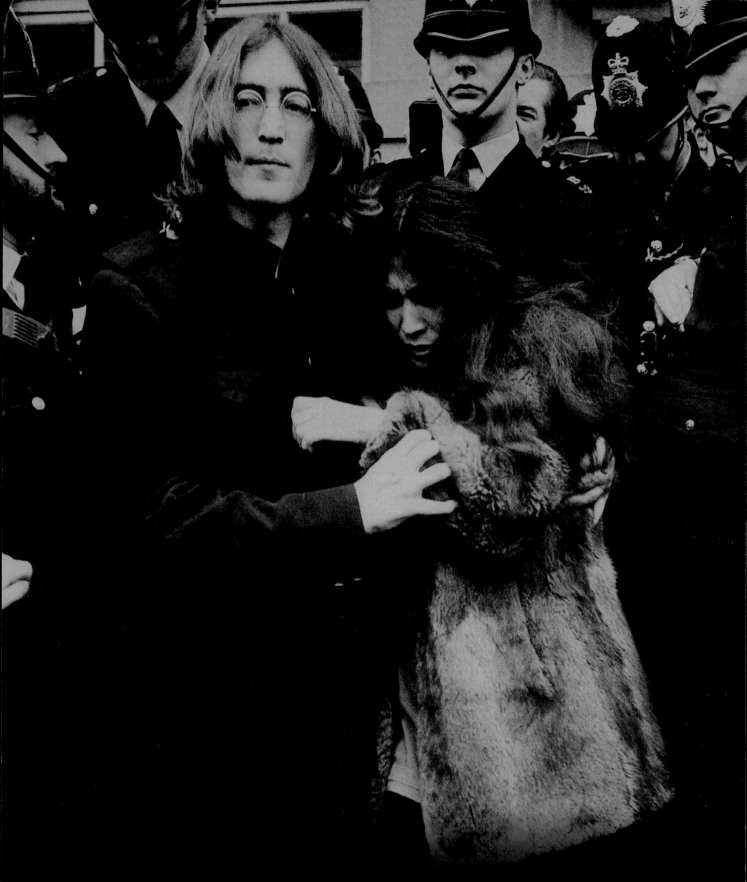

Beatle Lennon and Yoko face drug charges

Saturday, October 19, 1968

Beatle John Lennon and his girlfriend, Yoko Ono, were charged yesterday with possessing drugs and obstructing the police. They will appear in court today.

Scotland Yard detectives arrested them at Lennon's West End flat and took them to Paddington Green police station. They were charged with possessing cannabis resin and with obstructing police in the execution of a search warrant.

Eight detectives and a woman police constable in plain clothes had arrived at Lennon's ground-floor flat in Marylebone at lunchtime.

With them were two Labrador police dogs, specially trained to sniff out drugs.

They spent some time inside before Yoko – Japanese-born wife of American film producer Anthony Cox – appeared, dressed in a short fur coat and black trousers.

The policewoman escorted her down the three steps to the pavement where she was ushered into a small blue saloon car.

A few moments later Lennon walked out, accompanied by two detectives and wearing a Chinese-style black hip-length jacket and dark bell-bottom trousers. He got into the back of a white Mini.

They spent nearly two hours at the police station before being released on bail. They left by a side entrance.

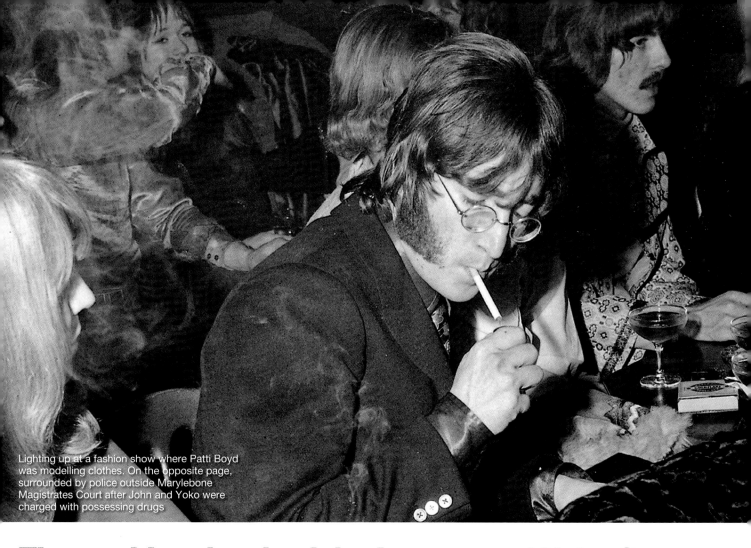

Lighting up at a fashion show where Patti Boyd was modelling clothes. On the opposite page, surrounded by police outside Marylebone Magistrates Court after John and Yoko were charged with possessing drugs

The world and us by John Lennon and Yoko Ono

Saturday, October 26, 1968

It's hard to tell the love story of John Lennon and Yoko Ono and of how they want to marry and have many more kids than the one they are happily expecting now.

Because they live in a bizarre world, the majority of us are not able to digest or accept – and that makes them freaks, doesn't it?

And like the people we call freaks, they don't do things we can easily understand. So they are regarded as eccentric and people believe they must be, because they would rather wear any old garb than conventional dress.

John Lennon suffers from this kind of ridicule more than Yoko, probably because we've known him longer, loved him and shared his fame.

Now it's widely said he has blown it all. You've heard it, I've heard it. And don't imagine that John Lennon hasn't heard it, too.

"I've blown my top, isn't that the word?" says John, without surprise or anger. "That my thinking has gone wrong and all the things I've got into have put me in disgrace.

"If I am to believe that, what should I do? Send my MBE back to the Queen?"

John Lennon, the witty Beatle who has always scored with the off-the-cuff gag, wasn't joking.

He meant it. Because he is not happy to think that public opinion should turn against him.

Now John is shunned – and even the most loyal Beatles fans are having their faith tested.

First came the bewildering news that John and his wife Cynthia had separated.

Next emerged his strange companionship with this Japanese artist whom none of us knew. Then we saw them planting acorns for one another and putting on baffling art gallery exhibitions with balloons and blank canvases.

Which brings us to last week's tragic event, when they were both arrested on a charge of possessing pot. The world of John Lennon looked about to collapse.

Here it is simply – John Lennon and Yoko Ono fell in love with one another. They had no right to because they were married.

Says Yoko: "We've suffered the same heartaches and problems as any other couple when this kind of thing happens.

"Unfortunately the public still want to see John as a pop star. But he's a tough man of 28 and he's got to be allowed to cross the gap."

Said John: "I've never known love like this before, and it hit me so hard that I had to halt my marriage to Cyn. And don't think that was a reckless decision because I felt deeply about it all and the implications that would be involved."

Cynthia has filed a divorce petition against John which the couple will not defend. Yoko's husband, American film producer Anthony Cox, is also to seek a dissolution of his marriage.

"When we are free – and we hope this will be within a year – we shall marry," said John.

They met two years ago when the Japanese girl came to London from America to stage a two-week exhibition of her concept art.

John was at the gallery before it opened. She invited him to hammer a nail into a picture.

"I honestly didn't know who he was. I had only heard of the name 'Beatles' and I'd heard of Ringo. But I immediately knew that here was someone who thought the same way as I did."

Their romance developed from there…John went off to India with Cynthia to meditate with the Maharishi.

"While I was there I wrote to Yoko," he said. "But at the time it was in a business sense. I had ideas to record her as an artist."

On his return to London, when he was reunited with Yoko, "the buzzings between us grew louder. Cyn asked me whether it was Yoko. I stalled because I wasn't sure. But when I knew the answer I sent a friend to tell my wife in Italy, where she had gone on holiday."

The Beatle has now come to a financial settlement with Cynthia and they have both agreed on the upbringing of their son, Julian.

"Some may say my decision was selfish," explained John. "Well, I don't think it is. Are your children going to thank you when they are 18? There is something else to consider, too – isn't it better to avoid rearing children in the atmosphere of a strained relationship?

"My marriage to Cyn was not unhappy. But it was just a normal marital state where we continued to sustain. You sustain it until you meet someone who suddenly sets you alight.

"With Yoko I really knew love for the first time. Our first attraction was a mental one, but it also happened physically. I never thought I'd marry again. Now the thought of it is so easy."

John's paper plane takes flight during a visit to the Guildford School of Art, December 1968. In the top picture, he and Yoko join the Rolling Stones' Rock 'n' Roll Circus, featuring Bill Wyman, Charlie Watts, Brian Jones, Keith Moon (The Who) and Eric Clapton (Cream). Opposite, the newly-married Lennons show off their marriage certificate in Gibraltar

The Lennons – in honeymoon gear

Friday, March 21, 1969

The marriage of Beatle John Lennon and his Japanese girlfriend Yoko Ono yesterday was, predictably, an unconventional affair.

They chartered an aircraft in Paris and, after sitting up talking all night, flew to Gibraltar for the three-minute ceremony – then flew right back again.

Yoko, 36, wore a white mini-dress and tennis shoes for the wedding. John wore white tennis shoes, too.

At Le Bourget airport John, 28, said: "It was all very quick, quiet and British.

"We have been trying to get married since last Friday. First of all we tried to marry on a cross-Channel ferry.

"Unfortunately, they have stopped that sort of thing on the ferries. Too many people were getting married and all the officers were so busy they had nobody to drive the ship."

The special licence for the Gibraltar wedding was arranged through solicitors in London – and not even the other Beatles were told of the plans.

The Lennons start a week-long lie-in

Wednesday, March 26, 1969

John Lennon and Yoko Ono, his new bride, took to their bed yesterday for the 'special happening' they promised would surprise the world.

And that, really, was that. For the only surprise was that they did practically nothing at all, except clutch a tulip each.

They plan to stay that way for seven days. Just sitting around in bed as a protest against war and violence in the world.

Many of the 200 reporters and photographers who filed through their £20-a-day suite at the Hilton Hotel in Amsterdam were puzzled at first.

John – reading their thoughts – said: "I hope it's not a let-down. We wouldn't make love in public – that's an emotionally personal thing."

In his white pyjamas, the 28-year-old Beatle said: "This is our protest against all the suffering and violence in the world." Yoko, 36, wearing a white, high-necked, old-fashioned nightie, said: "We want to tell the youth of the world that we are with them."

Above: The famous bed-in to promote world peace begins in the Hilton Hotel, Amsterdam

John Lennon sends his MBE back to the Queen

Wednesday, November 26, 1969

Beatle John Lennon sent his MBE medal back to the Queen yesterday – wrapped in an envelope and delivered to Buckingham Palace in his white Mercedes. With it was a letter to the Queen explaining why he was returning the award, which he received with the other Beatles in 1965.

The letter said: "I am returning my MBE as a protest against Britain's involvement in the Nigeria-Biafra thing, against our support of America in Vietnam and against 'Cold Turkey' slipping down the charts."

A copy of the letter has been sent to the Prime Minister, Harold Wilson.

Last night, John, with his wife by his side, said: "I feel very strongly about peace. This gesture is really a publicity gesture for peace."

Above: John is attempting to hide an injury at Dalcross Airport in Inverness after he and Yoko had a car accident while on holiday in Scotland, July 1969. Beatles' assistant Peter Brown is carrying Yoko's daughter, Kyoko.
Left: John stares straight into the camera after returning his MBE, November 1969

Dressed all in black at Heathrow before a trip to Toronto, December 1969. On the opposite page, the Lennons protest against the execution of James Hanratty, who was hanged in 1962 for the 'A6' murder the previous year. They are pictured with members of Hanratty's family

Paul quits the Beatles

Friday, April 10, 1970

Paul McCartney has quit the Beatles. The shock news must mean the end of Britain's most famous pop group, which has been idolised by millions the world over for nearly 10 years.

Today 27-year-old McCartney will announce his decision, and the reasons for it, in a no-holds-barred statement.

It follows months of strife over policy in Apple, the Beatles' controlling organisation, and an ever-growing rift between McCartney and his songwriting partner, John Lennon.

McCartney and Lennon are rated one of the greatest popular songwriting teams of the century. But there is little doubt that McCartney's decision will bring it to an end.

In his statement, which consists of a series of answers to questions, McCartney says: "I have no future plans to record or appear with the Beatles again. Or to write any more music with John."

Last night the statement was locked up in a safe at Apple headquarters in Savile Row, Mayfair, in the rooms where the Beatles' break-up began.

The Beatles decided to appoint a business adviser. Eventually they settled for American Allen Klein.

His appointment was strongly resisted by Paul, who sought the job for his father-in-law, American attorney Lee Eastman.

After a meeting in London Paul was out-voted 3-1 by John and the other Beatles, George Harrison and Ringo Starr.

Close friends tried to pacify John and Paul. But August last year was the last time they were to work together – when they collaborated on the 'Abbey Road' album.

Dick James, managing director of Northern Songs, publishers of the Lennon-McCartney songs, told me: "It could mean that in competition with each other they will write even greater songs. They are both geniuses – Paul a melodic one and John in an inventive capacity."

Opposite: John plays live (with the Plastic Ono Band) for the first time since 1966, at the Lyceum Theatre in London, December 1969. Yoko is in the bag. Above, the Lennons are pictured with black power activist Michael X in February 1970. John is holding locks of his and Yoko's newly-shorn hair, which were auctioned for the 'Black House' commune in London. The blood-stained shorts were donated by Muhammad Ali

Beatle Lennon gets a skinhead haircut

Wednesday, January 21, 1970

John Lennon, the hairiest pop apostle of them all, has joined the shaven ranks of the skinheads.

Today, where those famous Beatle locks once blossomed, there's nothing but bristle. He hasn't got a hair on his head more than an inch and a half long.

The most sensational scalping since the Indians went peaceful was carried out with great furtiveness during a visit to Denmark.

From a hideout in a deserted farm near the little Danish village of Vujt, he sent out the ominous request for a barber.

Aaje Haukrogh, a 27-year-old hairdresser from the nearby town of Aalburg, was chosen to execute the haircut of the decade.

Aaje said later: "I was just told to take a taxi to the farm to cut the hair of all five people there."

They included Yoko's wife, Yoko Ono, and her daughter by her previous marriage.

"It was quite an experience," said Aaje. "John said he was very satisfied when I'd finished."

Lennon said: "I want to be able to walk around unnoticed."

THE NEW YORK YEARS

After the Beatles split up, John embarked on a solo career and, in 1971, left Britain for America. The 1970s would be a turbulent decade for the Lennons

John and Yoko are arrested

Saturday, April 24, 1971

Beatle John Lennon and his wife Yoko Ono were being held by police last night for questioning over the alleged abduction of Yoko's seven-year-old daughter.

The couple were detained in Palma, Majorca.

They were being questioned by a magistrate who will decide whether there is a charge to answer.

Lennon and Yoko were taken to the magistrate's court after a complaint by Yoko's former husband, American film producer Anthony Cox.

Cox, who is staying in a hotel in Majorca, claimed that his daughter Kyoko had been snatched from a playground.

Police were reported to have found Kyoko at the Melia-Mallorca Hotel with her mother and Lennon.

The girl was taken in a police car to the court with the couple.

At the court later Lennon said: "I'm not exactly being detained. I'm trying to sort this matter out."

When the child disappeared Cox was attending a meditation session conducted by the Indian guru Maharishi, former spiritual adviser to the Beatles.

Court sources said that Lennon and his wife flew to Majorca to discuss Kyoko's return to her mother, but Cox was determined to keep the child.

Yoko was divorced from Cox in 1968.

We'll fight for Yoko's daughter, says Lennon

Monday, April 26, 1971

John Lennon and Yoko Ono were planning last night to fight a legal battle over the custody of Yoko's seven-year-old daughter, Kyoko.

In Majorca, scene of the drama of the alleged abduction of Kyoko, Yoko said: "I will be back for her, wherever she is, but now we must get a legal ruling."

Beatle John and his wife flew from Palma to Paris on Saturday night for talks with their lawyers.

They had spent nearly 14 hours at a Palma police station while a magistrate investigated the abduction charge made by Kyoko's father, American film producer Anthony Cox.

The magistrate ordered that the child should go with Cox – Yoko's former husband.

Before the couple left for Paris they talked about the affair.

Yoko asked: "How can you kidnap your own baby? I did what any mother would have done. I saw my child in a playground and she ran into my arms."

Lennon said: "We came here quite openly. How could we kidnap Kyoko when her father holds her passport? It's too ridiculous.

"It has taken us the last two years to nail down Kyoko's whereabouts. We heard accidentally through friends so we came out here to see her.

"We have done everything we can to come to an amicable agreement with her father and in all it's cost us over £50,000 and a shoal of broken promises. Yoko loves her daughter and I can't let her suffer this stress any longer."

Lennon, himself the child of a broken home, added: "What effect can all this be having on Kyoko? I remember it happening to me when I was three or four. I was shattered."

Left: John and Yoko in Majorca in April 1971, where they were arrested in a dispute over the custody of her daughter, Kyoko

Below: In their Greenwich Village apartment, which was their first home when they moved to New York in 1971

Above: The strain shows following the controversy over Kyoko, May 1971

Opposite page: A couple of poses, and a big hat

A relaxed pose at Heathrow
Airport in July 1971

Above: Getting off a bus
at Heathrow

Signing copies of Yoko's book 'Grapefruit' at Selfridges, July 1971

John's final headlining
concert appearance – at
Madison Square Garden,
New York, in August 1972
(see also overleaf)

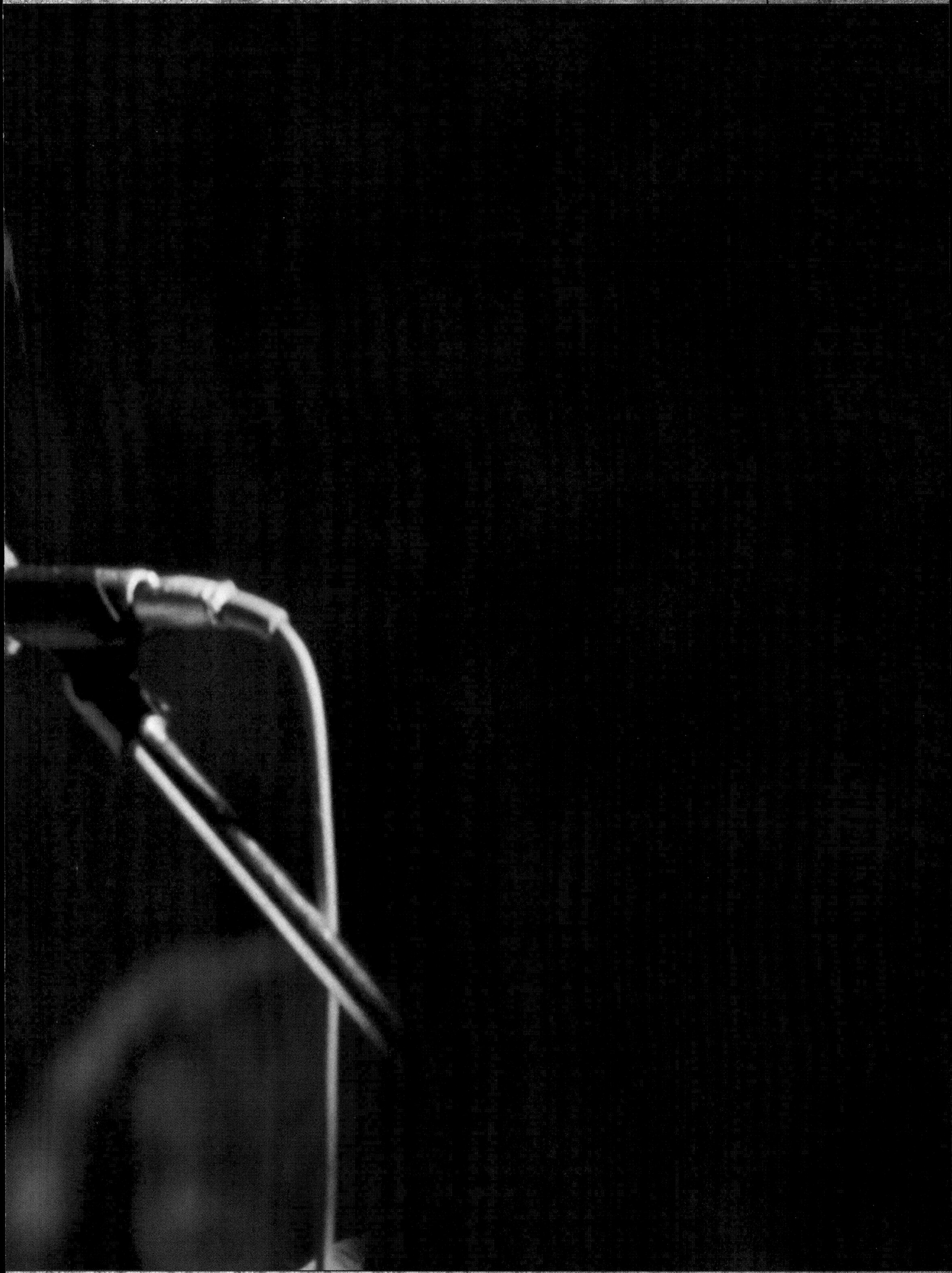

Pictured poolside at a friend's house in Beverly Hills, California, during his separation from Yoko, 1974

Opposite: A solitary man, relaxing and playing guitar

Beat it! US kick out John Lennon

Friday, February 14, 1975

America ordered former Beatle John Lennon out of the country yesterday.

He was told to quit because of a previous drugs conviction in Britain.

And it left Lennon, 32 and his Japanese-born wife, Yoko One, with an agonising decision.

For Yoko was given permission to stay in the US permanently. This means she could continue the long search for her missing daughter, Kyoko, by a previous marriage.

But it would also mean that Lennon and his wife, who were married four years ago, would have to part.

The couple were given custody of nine-year-old Kyoko by a Texas court a year ago.

But Kyoko and her father, film-maker Anthony Cox, vanished.

A massive search by police and private detectives has failed to trace them.

Lennon was given 60 days to get out of the country. The couple have been fighting for 13 months to stay in America since their visitors' visas expired.

Lennon's conviction in 1968 for possessing cannabis made him ineligible for permanent residence under America's immigration laws.

An immigration spokesman denied yesterday that the Lennons were being "victimised".

He said: "We have undertaken deportation proceedings hundreds of times in similar cases. Personal feelings don't come into it. We have the law to enforce."

The Lennons were believed to be somewhere on America's west coast.

Friends said they felt that if Lennon had to leave America, Yoko would go with him.

Lennon and Yoko get together again

Friday, February 14, 1975

Former Beatle John Lennon and his wife, Yoko Ono, were back together last night after a year-long 'trial' separation.

The couple will celebrate their reunion today with a St Valentine's party at their plush New York apartment overlooking Central Park.

When they split up, Lennon moved out of the apartment into a bachelor flat in Manhattan.

A happy Lennon described the separation as a "failure".

He told a friend: "We need each other and have decided to try again."

America 'ready to accept Lennon'

Sunday, June 15, 1976

Pop star John Lennon may be allowed to stay in the United States indefinitely, a top newspaperman claimed yesterday.

The ex-Beatle has been fighting deportation since 1972 after being branded an undesirable because of a 1968 charge in Britain for possessing marijuana.

Columnist Jack Anderson said that Lennon has a better-than-even chance of staying in America.

He said Watergate-like tactics had been used against Lennon.

They involved a smear-campaign by a Senate sub-committee that falsely linked Lennon with militants alleged to be plotting to disrupt the 1972 Republican convention.

An attorney has persuaded the Federal prosecutor that hundreds of aliens with worse drug records than Lennon have been allowed to stay.

Above: Outside a New York court in 1976 after winning his four-year legal battle to stay in America

John: Table for two on a rare night out

Monday, March 31, 1980

The diners at the chic, ultra-expensive Petite Marmite restaurant in Palm Beach were the usual crowd.

They hardly gave a passing glance to the odd couple sitting in the corner. With his swept back hair, full beard, thick-lensed glasses and tight, narrow-lapelled suit, he looked like an undernourished Russian novelist, or a quirkish professor.

She had long, tangled, dark hair and, despite the semi-gloom of the restaurant, hid behind dark glasses. She was still obviously Japanese.

John Lennon, now 39, and his wife Yoko Ono, 47, were on a very rare night out.

They are newcomers to the plush Palm Beach retirement belt. They seldom move out of the heavily-barricaded house, even to have a paddle in the sea, or sit in the sun on their private beach.

What do they do all day? Probably just what they do when they are in New York.

John, it seems, would just sit around. Sometimes he would bake a loaf of bread and contemplate the philosophical meaning of rising dough.

Other times, he might paint. Or write a poem. Something to do with the meaning of life. Or not, as the case may be.

He'd play with his four-year-old son, Sean. Or, if the mood took them, John and Yoko would just make love.

To John Lennon, a complex, highly eccentric man, money has no meaning. Of course, it does help if you can pick up an estimated £5 million a year on assorted royalties on songs you wrote and records you made. Then you can afford your own special outlook.

Last year he paid £10,000 for a full-page advert in the New York Times to inform a world breathless with anticipation that he and Yoko were truly in love.

Not so long ago he announced that he never intends to work again because he has "made my contribution to civilisation".

The man who has so much talent, and gave so much pleasure with his music and still has so much to give, has crawled back into his reality-insulated shell.

A happy family: John, Yoko and Sean, who was born in 1975

Opposite: Leaving The Hit Factory recording studio in New York, summer 1980

John and Yoko back at work

Thursday, August 14, 1980

Former Beatle John Lennon and his wife Yoko Ono are making music again. John and Yoko started recording their first album for seven years at The Hit Factory in New York.

One of the musicians working with the couple said: "It's Lennon's best to date. We're all very excited."

Lennon comes out of hiding

Thursday, October 9, 1980

Today John Winston Lennon celebrates his 40th birthday by saying goodbye to his nickname, Hermit of New York.

He has launched a new LP and a new career, marking the end of five years' seclusion.

Two words can sum up why the gaunt, five o'clock shadow man, once the most brilliant Beatle, locked himself away from prying eyes.

He's weird.

Multi-millionaire Lennon has done many strange things in his life. He appeared naked on a record sleeve – with his wife also naked – proving what a great boon clothes have been to mankind.

He has turned on his old Beatles wacker Paul McCartney at his front door in New York with the greeting: "Look, d'ya mind ringing first?"

He has sent acorns to heads of state as peace offerings and for the last five years he has baked bread, been a house-husband and never visited a rock club.

John and Yoko Ono have five dairy farms, five flats overlooking Central Park in New York and half a dozen other choice retreats from Florida to a mountain hideaway.

But now Lennon has resurfaced with what has been trumpeted as the most eagerly awaited album of the year.

It's called 'Double Fantasy', composed by Lennon and Yoko, the girl he married 11 years ago, took to Amsterdam for a week's honeymoon and spent all the time sitting on a bed talking about peace.

Then, in 1975, John and Yoko did a vanishing act. He holed himself up in his New York apartment behind marble walls and bodyguards.

Little Sean Lennon was the culprit, born after miscarriages gave Yoko only one more chance to have a child.

Lennon explained his seclusion recently: "I wanted to give Sean five solid years. I hadn't seen Julian, my first son, grow up at all, and now there's a 17-year-old man on the telephone talking about motorbikes."

So for years John Lennon's spotlight was on the kitchen sink, his only audience a helpless baby. Now it's back to the limelight. Why? John says: "Because this housewife would love to have a career for a bit! Now that Sean's five I can say: 'Daddy's does something else as well.'"

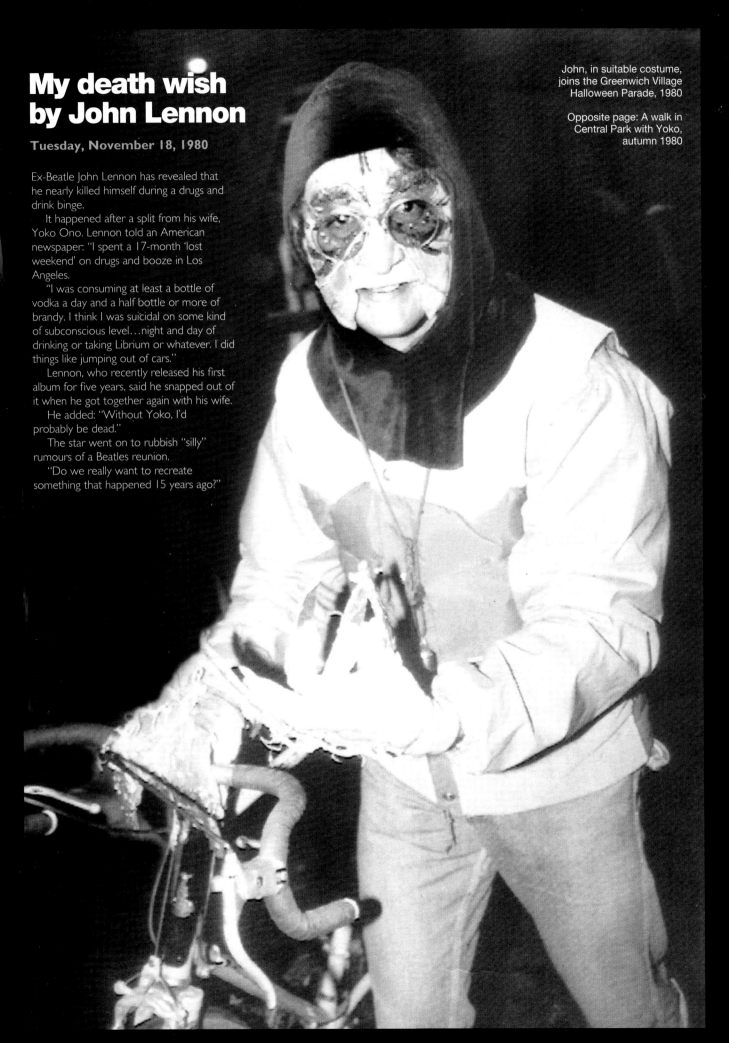

My death wish by John Lennon

Tuesday, November 18, 1980

Ex-Beatle John Lennon has revealed that he nearly killed himself during a drugs and drink binge.

It happened after a split from his wife, Yoko Ono. Lennon told an American newspaper: "I spent a 17-month 'lost weekend' on drugs and booze in Los Angeles.

"I was consuming at least a bottle of vodka a day and a half bottle or more of brandy. I think I was suicidal on some kind of subconscious level…night and day of drinking or taking Librium or whatever. I did things like jumping out of cars."

Lennon, who recently released his first album for five years, said he snapped out of it when he got together again with his wife.

He added: "Without Yoko, I'd probably be dead."

The star went on to rubbish "silly" rumours of a Beatles reunion.

"Do we really want to recreate something that happened 15 years ago?"

John, in suitable costume, joins the Greenwich Village Halloween Parade, 1980

Opposite page: A walk in Central Park with Yoko, autumn 1980

THE DAY
THE MUSIC DIED

On December 9, 1980 a horrified Britain woke up to discover that one of its heroes had been killed in New York. The death of John Lennon remains difficult to comprehend

Do you know what you've done?

Wednesday, December 10, 1980

With a nod that was almost friendly, John Lennon gave his autograph to the stocky young man carrying his latest album.

It was like signing his own death warrant. The polite, leather-jacketed fan went away with the prized signature, but hours later he again approached the pop idol.

This time the man wore a smirk and there was a menace in his voice. "Hey, Mr Lennon," he called. Then, without waiting for an answer, he struck a combat stance and emptied five bullets from a .38 revolver into the ex-Beatle's chest.

As Lennon cried out: "I've been shot, I've been shot," and slumped at the feet of his hysterical wife, Yoko One, the killer calmly threw his murder weapon down.

It clattered to the floor at the entrance to the Lennons' luxury New York apartment in front of the stunned doorman, who screamed: "Do you know what you've done?"

Still grinning, the killer retorted: "Yeah, I just shot John Lennon."

If his motive was to make himself as infamous as Lennon was famous, he succeeded.

Within hours of Lennon's violent death at 10.50pm local time – 3.50am

British time yesterday – the name of Mark David Chapman was known throughout the world.

As Yoko cradled her husband's bullet-ridden body in a police car rushing him to hospital, she sobbed: "Tell me it isn't true."

Tragically, it was. At the age of 40 the brilliant Liverpool-born composer, whose lasting theme for the world was love and peace, lay dead at her side.

His wish to die before his wife was fulfilled almost as soon as he spoke of it.

In an interview only hours before his death, he said: "I hope to die before Yoko because if she died I wouldn't know how to survive. I couldn't carry on."

If Yoko didn't know the worst, confirmation was not long in coming.

From the police car, officers carried Lennon's stretcher into an emergency room at New York's Roosevelt Hospital.

Alongside them a doctor tried feverishly to restart the star's heart with hand massage. But it was too late.

"Please, no. Please, no. Please, no," screamed Yoko as she realised the truth.

Suddenly everyone waiting for treatment in that emergency ward knew who had just died.

Later, back at their lavish home in the Dakota apartment block overlooking Manhattan's Central Park, a more composed Yoko issued a statement which said simply: "John loved and prayed for the human race. Please do the same for him."

Outside, candles were lit. Thousands of shocked, disbelieving Beatles' followers were staging an amazing wake.

Flowers, sprays of mixed blooms and single roses were attached to the giant wrought-iron gates through which the killer had slipped a few hours earlier.

The strains of the gentle refrain that Lennon and Yoko made their own special message to the world – 'All we are saying, is give peace a chance' – wafted on the early-morning air.

People of all ages and colours wept and hugged each other in the way that Lennon once preached. Even police took part in the ceremony of instant mourning, after sealing the road off to traffic.

The song changed.

Softly, the cruelly telling lyrics of 'Yesterday' built up.

Then a middle-aged man switched on a cassette recorder which echoed other Beatles numbers.

At dawn, six hours after the shooting, hundreds of mourners still knelt outside the building reciting prayers. A colour picture of Lennon was on the fence. Flowers littered the pavement.

News of their hero's shooting had shocked millions.

All-night radio stations burst into non-stop musical tributes. Some disc jockeys wept as they read the tragic bulletin.

Last night it was revealed that Lennon had been warned to quit violent New York weeks before his murder.

Friends feared for his safety as he stepped back into public life after living like a hermit for five years.

The rock star refused to move to California. He said New York's vitality overcame its violence and it reminded him more of Liverpool, the other waterfront city where his success story was born.

Millions mourn an idol who changed their world

Wednesday, December 10, 1980

Grief for John Lennon was shared yesterday by everyone who knew him – and by countless millions who did not.

One of the first people in Britain to learn of his killing was his former wife Cynthia, the mother of his 17-year-old son Julian. The news was broken to her before dawn by Ringo Starr's ex-wife Maureen, after the former Beatles drummer phoned her from the Bahamas.

Cynthia, who had been visiting Maureen in Surrey, left immediately to be with Julian and her husband, restaurateur John Twist, at their home in Ruthin, North Wales.

Cynthia said in tears: "We are all terribly upset by John's sudden and tragic death. I have always held John in the deepest regard since our divorce and encouraged the relationship between him and Julian."

Later Cynthia and her husband took Julian to Heathrow Airport and he flew to New York.

Julian, who was clearly showing his distress, told reporters he wanted to follow in his father's footsteps as a musician.

In Britain, Paul McCartney and George Harrison were stunned by John's death.

Paul told reporters: "I can't take it in at the moment. He is going to be missed by the whole world."

George said: "I have great love and respect for John. I am shocked and stunned. It's such a terrible waste."

In New York Ringo hurried with his girlfriend, Barbara Bach, to see Yoko after they flew in from the Bahamas.

A friend said: "He's very shocked. He doesn't want to speak."

Tributes poured in from pop stars who had been inspired by Lennon's music.

Rolling Stone Mick Jagger said: "I'm absolutely stunned. I knew and liked John for 18 years. But I don't want to make a casual remark about him now at such an awful moment for his family and millions of fans and friends."

Roger Daltrey, lead singer of The Who, said: "It's terrible. My heart goes out to his family, wife and sons."

Radio and TV stations all over the world paid tribute to him last night.

BBC TV changed their programmes to screen tributes and the old Beatles film 'Help'.

Opposite page: The last picture of John Lennon, autographing his latest album for Mark Chapman
Left: A fan lights a candle in memory of her hero

Image: Police examine the scene of the shooting. Bullet holes are visible in the glass on the door

Right: A distraught Yoko on the night her husband was killed

All you need is love

Wednesday, December 10, 1980

Love made the crazy world go round for John Lennon and his wife, Yoko Ono. They were the odd couple – sometimes shocking, sometimes baffling. But always fascinating. And passionately in love.

Japanese artist Yoko changed Lennon's life. They parted, only to find that they could not live without each other.

Yoko was born 47 years ago, the daughter of a Japanese banker who went to live in New York when she was a child.

"I used to have to make an appointment to see my father," she recalls. "I always went for the opposite type of men, a man who had insecurities."

Yoko met Lennon in a London art gallery in November 1966. She had an immediate impact on the Beatle.

He was to say: "She forced me to become avant garde and take my clothes off when all I wanted was to become Tom Jones."

They were married secretly in Gibraltar in 1969 and later had an 'open house' honeymoon, inviting everyone to walk in and see them in their double bed.

Then Lennon and Yoko set out to make their mark on the youth movement of the early '70s.

Drawings of their love-making went on sale. They even posed nude for the cover of an LP.

In 1975 their son Sean was born and Lennon faded from the public eye. He became a house-husband, staying at home to look after Sean while Yoko went to the office to deal with their multi-million pound business. Lennon baked bread in their New York flat and in their retreat in the Catskill Mountains.

On October 9 there was a double anniversary – Lennon's 40th birthday and his son's fifth.

For his presents, John and Yoko gave Sean a £62,500 plane, complete with pilot. Yoko also hired a plane to write 'Happy Birthday' across the New York skyline.

It was to be a new beginning, celebrating the famous couple's love in song.

Lennon went back to work happily. The result was the album 'Double Fantasy' and the hit single 'Starting Over'.

Yoko told an interviewer after the records were released that Starting Over carried a message of Lennon's optimism for the future.

"He's reaching out to me, the woman, reaching out after all that's happened," she said.

Last night Yoko was locked up in her mansion flat with her son and her memories.

An upset fan listens to Beatles' songs outside the Dakota

John cremated in secret as Yoko mourns

Thursday, December 11, 1980

John Lennon was cremated yesterday in extraordinary secrecy.

Not even his wife , Yoko Ono, was present. It was feared that she might be spotted leaving her apartment by the massive crowds of fans and newsmen waiting outside.

Lennon's body was released from the public morgue before dawn.

It was taken to a Manhattan funeral parlour and cremated at noon – 5pm British time.

Yoko had announced that there would be no funeral for her murdered husband.

"Instead," she said. "We will set the time for a silent vigil to pray for his soul."

Her lawyers also feared that a funeral could be turned into a huge display of mass hysteria by Lennon's grief-stricken followers.

Comfort is offered amongst the crowd gathered on 72nd Street

Vigil on 72ⁿᵈ Street

Thursday, December 11, 1980

The flowers never stopped coming. They stood in big bunches where they had been propped against the wall, and they lost their petals slowly in the rain which hurled down and made glistening floods in the gutters.

Small bunches washed over 72nd Street. The clouds put their own grey wreaths around the tops of Manhattan's great buildings.

New York now has a new shrine. People came through the night as pilgrims out of the leafless woods of Central Park, and stood dripping like so many dark statues in a fountain.

Through the iron gates across the entrance to the Dakota building, mostly hidden by the high drift or carnations and red roses, a doorman stood in his uniform and his brass buttons shone in the lights of the cars.

From somewhere between the speckled lights of candles, which people lit and shielded in their supped hands, the Beatles' saddest songs moaned out of the radios which picked the music from practically every station.

Then there were kids sobbing, going on their knees to pray.

Policewoman Giles tucked the straightened ends of her hair under her hat again and shuffled like a mourner among the crowds on 72nd Street.

"I volunteered – I had to be there," she said. "I've cried for hours."

There was no spark in New York. The city had died. Some warped kid had killed John Lennon and New York put its head down in shame.

The night slipped on, snow came down with the rain. The cops kept the crowds in line and an ambulance took away some girl in hysteria.

Then somebody else began screaming, then a group of girls were screaming. The cops moved in with shiny wet coats and calmed things.

There was wailing at the gates to the Dakota. The sound filled the street for minutes, then stopped and the music was everywhere again. "Love is everything, love is everything, love is everything."

The lyrics died out on one radio and picked up on another. The Beatles were the only people on TV, the cameras zoomed in on John Lennon.

Not even the temperature falling to freezing shook the people out of the trances they had gone into outside the Dakota.

"See, they're still coming," policewoman Giles said. "It's going to be a landmark in this city. They're going to be coming here for ever."

At 11.07, the minute that John Lennon had died one day before, the crowd began to sing about peace again.

It was still going on when a picture of Lennon's body wrapped in a blue blanket was shown being wheeled away from the Roosevelt Hospital.

A girl collapsed in front of a car, and policewoman Giles went running over, telling somebody to get an ambulance.

The cops pulled their barricades across 72nd Street and sent the traffic way down Manhattan.

"Good God," one of the cops said to a colleague. "It's beginning to get to me now."

It was more than just another death on the streets of New York.

Where were you when John died?

Former Prime Minister Gordon Brown:
I will never forget it. I was lecturing at Edinburgh University when the news came through that he'd been shot. I remember playing his songs all that night.

Judy Finnigan:
I was a reporter working for Granada TV in Manchester. I had no chance to take it in before I was despatched to his first wife Cynthia's house to get her reaction. It was a tough thing to do but I had to be professional. All I remember her saying was "I'm very sad." It all seemed surreal and over the next few days the song 'Imagine' seemed to be playing everywhere. It was all so sad.

Bruce Springsteen:
I was in Philadelphia. I had to play that night, a very, very tough night to play. He made some amazing music on his own and was really quite out there on the frontier in a lot of things. He had had courage and humour. He was wonderful to have in the world – I'm still angry he's not here.

Tony Blackburn:
I was at home in London. I turned the TV on and there was the newsflash. I'd grown up with the Beatles and I'd met Lennon when I presented Top of the Pops. It was all such a shock.

Madonna:
I'd just moved to New York and was walking a few blocks away when I heard sirens and saw a crowd. I remember walking up and asking: "What's going on?" They said John Lennon was shot. It was so weird.

Lionel Richie:
I was on tour. We had just come offstage and someone came to me, they'd turned on the news and said: "John Lennon has been shot." I never thought of 'shot and wounded'. I knew they meant dead.

Jon Snow:
I was in Iran's capital, Tehran, covering the Iran hostage crisis. When the news broke, the hotel's concierge burst into tears.

EXCLUSIVE
By DAVID EDWARDS

WHEN five gunshots rang out in New York 25 years ago, they ended the life of one of the world's most influential musicians and sent millions of fans into mourning.

John Lennon had been living quietly in the city and had just made his comeback after five years away from the studio.

"John and I were gloriously happy in the first week of December," his widow later recalled. "In our minds, we were a team – old soldiers."

So exactly what happened on December 8, 1980? Here, we chart the final hours of the ex-Beatle and how he was targeted by Mark Chapman...

7.30am As the sun rises over Central Park, 40-year-old John Lennon gets out of bed and slips into his black kimono.

Leaving his wife, Yoko Ono, sleeping beneath the sheets, he creeps into the living room and stares out at the Manhattan skyline.

Yoko finds him lost in thought as sunlight floods into the stark, white-washed room.

Both are on a high. After five years out of the limelight, their new joint album, Double Fantasy, is riding high in the charts and they are busy recording a follow-up.

"What are we going to do when it's No.1, John?" Yoko asks.

"I'll take you out to dinner," he replies.

"That's a date?"

"That's a date."

Although the album went on to top charts around the world, John was never able to keep his promise...

Today is one of the warmest December days New Yorkers can remember. But John and Yoko don't have time to enjoy it – they have a full day's work ahead, including a photo session and a radio interview.

Meanwhile, 20 blocks across town, at the Sheraton Center Hotel on 7th Avenue, Mark David Chapman is also contemplating his day.

The security guard flew into the city two days ago intending to kill John Lennon. Over the weekend, he'd spent hours outside the Dakota building, where John and Yoko live.

9.00am John and Yoko leave the Dakota and have breakfast at the Cafe La Fortuna, on West 71st Street. John tucks into eggs benedict and follows it with a cappuccino and Gitane cigarette.

John then decides to have a haircut, after which the couple return to their sprawling 34-room apartment and welcome photographer Annie Leibovitz inside.

11.00am She asks John if he'd consider stripping off for the photo, while Yoko remains clothed. The resulting picture makes the front

9am
John and Yoko leave the Dakota building, passing the spot where he would be shot later that day

11am Photo shoot for Rolling Stone magazine cover

KILLER: Mark Chapman

cover of Rolling Stone magazine six weeks later.

1.00pm San Francisco radio producer Dave Sholin arrives to conduct what becomes John's last interview.

During the three-hour session, the musician poignantly says: "We're either going to live or we're going to die. I consider that my work won't be finished until I'm dead and buried – and I hope that's a long time."

5.00pm Sholin offers John and Yoko a lift to the recording studio. Outside the Dakota, the pavement teems with office workers heading for the subway. Among them is Mark Chapman, 25,

COMEBACK Lennon in his last days

Twenty-five years after his death, the Daily Mirror breaks down Lennon's last day

DAILY MIRROR, *Saturday, December 3, 2005* PAGE 19

Monday 8th December 1980

9.20am Having breakfast with Yoko at Cafe La Fortuna

Lennon's last day

5.05pm John signs Double Fantasy album cover watched by Mark Chapman

TRAGIC: John's body on a hospital trolley after his death

determined to kill Lennon, who he sees as a "phoney" – a left-wing activist with a millionaire lifestyle.

Despite the mild weather, Chapman wears thermal underwear, green trousers, a shirt and sweater, and a long green overcoat, complete with a fake fur hat, gloves and a green scarf.

A Charter Arms .38 snub-nosed revolver is concealed in the inside pocket of his coat.

He hands John a copy of Double Fantasy to sign. Wearing a black leather jacket over a blue sweater and red T-shirt, John writes: John Lennon 1980. Handing it back, he looks his killer in the eye and asks: "Here, is that what you want?" before hopping into the car.

John and Yoko, 47, spend four-and-a-half hours working at the Record Factory. John arranges to return at 9am the next day, turning to engineer Jack Douglas and smiling: "See

you tomorrow morning, bright and early!"

10.35pm Their limousine takes them up Eighth Avenue to Columbus Circle, continues north along Central Park West and then left into 72nd Street. On the way, John chats excitedly about saying goodnight to his five-year-old son, Sean.

Chapman is still loitering in front of the Dakota, where he's struck up a conversation with doorman José Perdomo.

10.48pm The limo stops outside the building's gateway and Yoko climbs out, followed by John carrying a tape recorder and

cassettes. John stares at Chapman as he passes by and, as he moves off, the killer springs into action...

Dropping into a combat stance, he pulls out the gun. The first two shots hit John in the back, spinning him around, while another two hit him in the shoulder. A fifth misses. Each bullet passes through the body and slams into a wood and glass windbreak behind him.

As Chapman looks on in silence, Lennon staggers up the five steps into the building's office, mumbling "I'm shot" before falling face-down. Night man Jay Hastings had been reading a magazine but, when John stumbles in, he hits the alarm button under the desk, summoning police.

Yoko rushes to cradle her dying husband and screams for a doctor.

Outside, Chapman removes his coat – so police will see he isn't armed – and begins flicking through his worn copy of JD Salinger's The Catcher In The Rye.

Within two minutes, the street is full of sirens. As Chapman is cuffed, two officers hoist the musician on to their shoulders and place him in the back of a squad car. Jay remembers hearing John's bones creak as they pick him up.

As his partner runs red lights heading to St Luke's Roosevelt Hospital Center, Officer James Moran turns and asks John: "Do you know who you are?" As he slips away, he nods and moans: "Yes." It is the last thing he ever says.

When John is wheeled into the emergency room, he has lost 80 per

cent of his blood and has virtually no pulse.

11.15pm Although seven medics have desperately tried to revive him, John is finally pronounced dead. The official cause is shock, produced by massive haemorrhaging.

Two days later, as the world mourns the senseless killing, his body is cremated at the Ferncliff Mortuary, in the suburb of Hartsfield.

Eight months later, Chapman, having pleaded guilty to murder, is sentenced to between 20 years and life in jail. Refused parole for the third time in October last year, he is held at Attica State Prison, New York.

Tellingly, prisoner 81A2860 is kept in solitary confinement for his own protection. Even the most hardened criminals in America would relish the chance to kill the man who killed one of music's greatest icons.

MONDAY: LENNON'S 15-MONTH 'LOST WEEKEND'

david.edwards@mirror.co.uk

LENNON'S LEGACY

There are memorials to John Lennon all over the world, most notably in his home city of Liverpool and adopted home, New York City, while both his sons carry the musical torch

Yoko Ono at Liverpool John Lennon Airport, named in his honour in 2002. The airport's motto, 'Above us only sky' is, of course, taken from 'Imagine'

Above and right: Yoko and Cherie Blair unveil the statue of Lennon that is situated within the airport building

Below: The Lennon statue that stands in Mathew Street, Liverpool, home of The Cavern, the club where the Beatles made their name. To the right is the 'Imagine' mosaic, a focal point of 'Strawberry Fields' in New York's Central Park

STRAWBERRY FIELDS

JOHN LENNON 1940-1980 Musician and Songwriter lived here 1945-1963

ENGLISH HERITAGE

The National Trust
No entry
For tour times and prices
please phone 0151 427 7231
or visit
www.spekehall.org.uk

Left and above: 'Mendips', 251 Menlove Avenue in Woolton, Liverpool, Lennon's childhood home, which is owned by the National Trust and has been open to the public since 2003. The top picture shows the 'Strawberry Fields' sign in Central Park

Above and below: John's two sons, Julian and Sean. Both are musicians